Our fur babies teach us how to love and also how to mourn.
They show us that happiness can be found in the most simplest things.

The loss of a 4-legged family member can be devastating, but I've always found comfort knowing that just like us, cats have a chance to go to a better place. A place filled with pure joy, unconditional love, and an endless supply of yummy treats! I hope this book not only comforts your family in times of heartache, but also reaffirms the promise of God's steadfast love for us all...including our furry friends!

Melanie Salas

but I'm happy that you now have wings to fly.

It helps to keep me from feeling so sad...

when I think about all the fun we had.

In Heaven, I bet there are a million places to run.

So,
even though
we had to say
goodbye.

And
I will know
as I see the
beautiful clouds
of white...

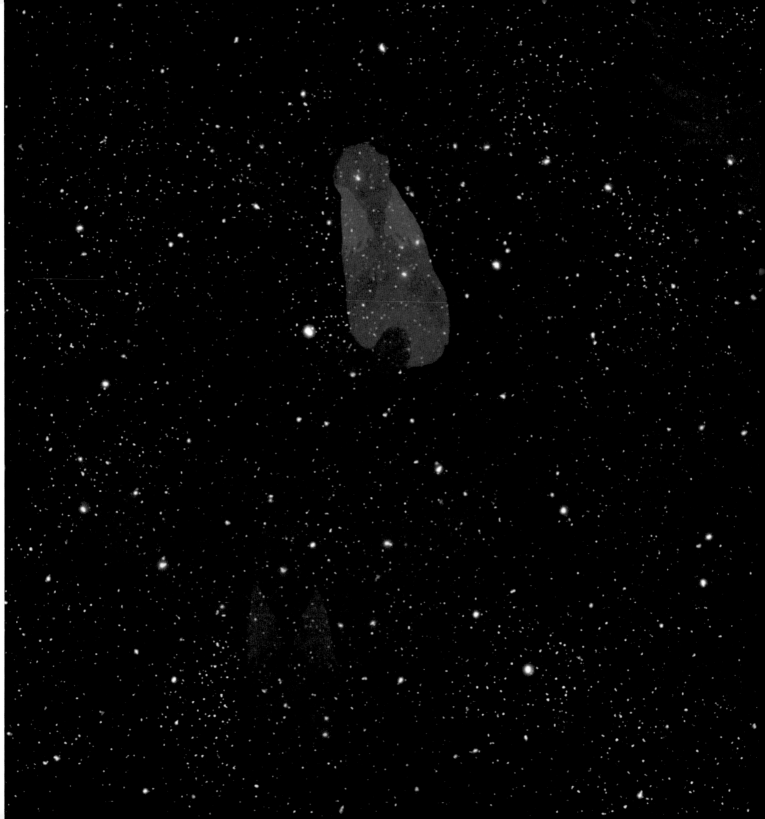

or the shining stars at night...

Cats in Heaven by Melanie Salas
Published by Golden Crown Publishing, LLC

www.GoldenCrownPublishing.com

© 2021 Golden Crown Publishing, LLC

All rights reserved. No portion of this book may be reproduced in any form without permission from the publisher, except as permitted by U.S. copyright law.
For permissions contact:
help@GoldenCrownPublishing.com

Created by Melanie Salas
ISBN:978-1-954648-47-0

Made in United States
Orlando, FL
26 October 2024